Original title:
The Ocean's Breath

Copyright © 2025 Creative Arts Management OÜ
All rights reserved.

Author: Adeline Fairfax
ISBN HARDBACK: 978-1-80581-662-1
ISBN PAPERBACK: 978-1-80581-189-3
ISBN EBOOK: 978-1-80581-662-1

Serenity in the Storm

Waves like giggles crash and roll,
Seaweed dances, plays a troll.
Fishes laugh in bubbles bright,
Jellyfish glide, a comical sight.

Seagulls squawk a silly tune,
Surfboards tumble, none too soon.
Children squeal as waves go splat,
Seashells hide, beneath a hat.

Thunder rumbles, skies turn gray,
Rain drops fall, and kids at play.
Umbrellas flip, a grand ballet,
Splashing puddles lead the way.

In chaos, joy begins to bloom,
Mermaids giggle, make some room!
Sandy cheeks with grins so wide,
In this storm, we'll laugh and glide.

Riptides of Reflection

Waves come in with a silly grin,
Pulling sandcastles down like a win.
Seagulls squawk, trying to steal my fries,
I dodge them swiftly, oh what a surprise!

Flip-flops flop while I run for my bliss,
Splashing water, can't resist that kiss.
Shells whisper secrets of jellyfish dances,
As I attempt awkward summer romances.

Devotions of the Deep

Fish in tuxedos swim past aloof,
A crab in a top hat thinks he's so smooth.
Sand dollars giggle, they've seen it all,
While clams hide inside their cozy shell hall.

A mermaid asks for a coffee break,
Sipping sea foam, oh what a mistake!
Neptune grumbles, where's my golden trident?
But he's too busy playing with the vibrant.

Sea Glass Musings

Pieces of glass, like treasures so rare,
Sun-kissed and polished, I stop and stare.
Why does the sea keep losing its gems?
Maybe it's just their quirky whims.

I ponder the waves and their silly game,
Offering trinkets but never the same.
I pick up a bottle, it gives me a wink,
It's empty, of course, not much left to drink!

Infinity in the Riptide

Riptides swirl with a laugh and a jig,
As I tumble and twist like a misfit twig.
"Surf's up!" my buddy shouts with delight,
But here I am, stuck in a watery fight.

Crabs hold a party, I'm not on the list,
They dance with jellyfish, oh how they twist!
I float past the fun, just a goofy sight,
Duck-diving dreams, oh what a mixed night!

Waves of Nostalgia

I found my flip-flops in the sand,
They danced around like they had a band.
Seashells whisper secrets of a feast,
But all I got was a sunburned beast.

The tide pulls back with tricks up its sleeve,
As crabs dance like jesters, I can't believe.
A seagull squawks, 'Hey, watch your snack!'
I turn around fast, my sandwich's back!

Echoes Beneath the Surface

Fishy friends play tag with my toes,
They giggle and poke, only heaven knows.
Bubbles rise up like a chorus of cheer,
But I just hope they don't notice my rear!

The water tickles, splashes with glee,
As I flop like a fish, in an awkward spree.
All the seaweed laughs as it wraps around,
My graceful swim turn a comedic bound!

Castaway Melodies

On a driftwood throne, I reign supreme,
With my coconut crown, living the dream.
A parrot squawks, 'Your style's a delight!'
But really I wish I could wear it at night.

Sandcastles tower, defying the flow,
While the tide crashes in, shouting, 'Just go!'
I yell back, 'Not my fault you're so rude!'
A battle of wills in this sandy mood!

When the Sea Sings Softly

The waves hum softly, a whimsical tune,
As jellyfish jiggle, plotting by noon.
A starfish claps, 'Encore, please!'
While I am just hoping my sunscreen won't freeze.

A sandpiper strolls, its strut full of flair,
It trips on a shell with a comical air.
The tide waves goodbye, with a wink and a cheer,
As I splash back home, shouting, 'Come here!'

Tide Pools and Treasure Hunts

In the tide pools, crabs do dance,
With tiny legs in a quirky prance.
Starfish lounge in the sandy sun,
Giggling softly—oh, what fun!

A lost shoe hides under a rock,
Snails play tag and laugh around the clock.
Shells whisper secrets of ocean lore,
While clams just snooze, snoring galore.

Kids with buckets scoop with glee,
Finding treasures for all to see.
Gooey seaweed, slippery and green,
Turns every toe into a slimy scene!

With giggles echoing on the shore,
Each splash is a chance for laughter galore.
The tide rolls in, then says goodbye,
As seagulls squawk and sail up high.

The Heartbeat of the Deep

Bubbles rise like laughter in a tub,
Fish play hide-and-seek, what a club!
Octopuses twist like silly dancers,
While manta rays glide with curious glances.

The deep sea tickles with its cool embrace,
Where jellyfish float with jelly-like grace.
A whale's song booms like a big deep joke,
It sends the tiny fish into a poke!

Clownfish chuckle behind the reef,
While squids compose fun-chores with a brief.
Lobsters hide with a snicker and glee,
Thinking of all the birthday parties at sea!

What would we find in this watery sprawl?
A dancing crab in a school's curtain call?
The heartbeat pulses, a rhythm of fun,
In the depths where laughter is never done.

Boundless Blue

The vast blue stretches, far and wide,
Where surfboards chase the joyful tide.
Seashells giggle as waves roll in,
While dolphins leap with a cheeky grin.

Oh, the fish throw a party today,
Wearing sunglasses, ready to play.
A sea turtle winks, slow and cool,
As a clown fish honks like a silly fool!

The horizon shimmers with vibrant hues,
Seagulls steal fries left by the crews.
With each wave, a fresh tale unfurls,
Of pirate dreams and treasure churl girls.

Boundless blue, with surprises and cheer,
Calls out to all who dare come near.
So grab a floatie, let laughter ensue,
In the world of whimsy, deep ocean blue!

The Canvas of Water

Watercolors splash in vibrant glee,
As waves paint smiles for all to see.
The canvas swirls with a playful tide,
While sea cucumbers just try to hide.

A crab in a top hat takes center stage,
While seaweed dancers flip and engage.
Starfish direct with their pincer applause,
In this underwater, whimsical cause.

Mermaids wave, with sparkly tails,
Sharing their stories of conspiratorial fails.
A fish dressed as a pirate shouts, "Avast!",
But trips on a rock, oh what a blast!

With laughter echoing in the salty air,
Each drop of paint tells a comical tale.
The canvas of water, forever anew,
With giggles and splashes, just waiting for you!

Shimmering Depths

The fish wear sunglasses, quite the sight,
They swim in circles, holding tight.
Seahorses dance, in a funny ball,
While crabs hold parties, they have a ball.

The jellyfish jiggles, so very bright,
Telling jokes that bring fish delight.
Underwater disco, bubbles fly,
They laugh and wiggle, oh my, oh my!

Lullaby of the Sea

The waves hum softly, a silly tune,
While seagulls swoop in a mad cartoon.
Starfish lay back, enjoying the breeze,
Making wishes, 'Oh, if you please!'

Fish in pajamas, what a sight,
Tickling dolphins, oh what a fright!
With every splash, there's a giggle or two,
As the tide sings softly, 'We love you!'

Solitudes of Sailboats

Sailboats drift with a lazy grin,
Chasing the sunset, oh what a win!
With wobbly sails, they laugh and sway,
Trying to catch the wind's playful play.

A crab on the bow, making a fuss,
Shouts, 'Hurry up, we're missing the bus!'
The captain shouts back, 'Hold your claws tight,
We'll reach the shore before it's night!'

The Art of Drift

Floating on waves, it's a neighborly art,
The sea turtles munch, a culinary part.
While otters juggle, with seaweed in tow,
Rolling and laughing, putting on a show!

The buoy keeps bobbing, it's quite a tease,
Waving to boats that float with ease.
Even the anchors seem to have fun,
Taking a break, hiding in the sun!

Whispers of the Tidal Symphony

Waves do the cha-cha on the shore,
Seagulls groove, they're never a bore.
Crabs play maracas, clickity-clack,
Starfish are partying, no looking back.

The sand is a dance floor, just wait and see,
The tide pulls us in like a cheeky spree.
Seashells are trumpets, they call us near,
With frothy cocktails made of sea foam beer.

Every splash a giggle, every crest a grin,
Dolphins are jesters, with antics and spins.
With jellyfish jumping, it's a true delight,
As the sun sets, we laugh till the night.

Currents of Forgotten Dreams

In the whirlpool, dreams do a dive,
Octopus chefs cook, oh how they thrive!
They serve up delights with a side of surprise,
Pufferfish popping, a feast for the eyes.

Sea turtles shuffle, doing the twist,
Forget about gravity, give it a mist.
The kraken has started a stand-up routine,
With a punchline or two, it's all quite obscene.

Anemones giggle in the bubbles below,
Clownfish clowning while kelp starts to flow.
The rhythm of currents, a laughter parade,
Forget all your worries, let fun be replayed.

Salty Serenade at Dusk

As the sun dips low, the stars start to torch,
Hermit crabs hustle, and take part in a porch.
The flip-flop sonata plays soft in the breeze,
While sandcastles crumbling say "Oh, pretty please!"

Gulls are crooning a melodious tune,
With fish in their sights, they swoop like a swoon.
The tide's softly humming, but wait for the twist,
Mermaids moonwalk, oh, you get the gist!

Laughter erupts with the splash of a fin,
While sea cucumbers sneak outside for a grin.
With each ebb and flow, the jokes ride the waves,
Tell me who doesn't love giggles like these?

A Horizon's Lullaby

In the eve, a whale sings a lullaby sweet,
As crabs tap dance, oh, they can't be beat.
Barnacles boast of adventures vast,
While fish play charades of their glorious past.

Tides tickle toes on the sandy expanse,
Kelp sways like dancers in an oceanic trance.
While seagulls serenade with a raucous delight,
And plankton do pirouettes in shimmering light.

Sunset's the moment for folly and flair,
As dolphins dish out the love and the care.
With every wave lapping, you know just who's wise,
It's all one great laugh beneath painted skies.

Rhythms of the Deep

Under waves where fish reside,
A crab does the limbo, full of pride.
Jellyfish boogie with soft grace,
While seahorses waltz in a slow race.

Seashells laugh in the salty breeze,
An octopus tickles, oh what a tease!
Starfish play cards on the sand below,
With laughter echoing in the undertow.

Dolphins dive into a silly spin,
With conch shells blaring—let the fun begin!
Sandcastles topple with each wild wave,
As crabs get caught in a clammy rave.

Fishes gossip about the day's show,
While the sea cucumber plays limbo too low.
With each splash, the surf's bubbling cheer,
The antics of the deep, oh so dear!

Currents of Serenity

The sea's a pool of laughter bright,
Where turtles race at morning light.
Seagulls shout with a funny squawk,
While fishes practice their best rock walk.

Wave after wave is a tickling spree,
And the little crabs form a funny teepee.
In this calm chaos, all creatures play,
While otters roll in a puff of spray.

Clams conspire in their shell-bound town,
While a lobster wears a goofy crown.
With starfish hosting a beach relay,
The currents swirl in a jolly way.

Above, the sun beams a golden grin,
As sea cucumbers start to spin.
In this joyful splash and silly cheer,
The ocean tickles both far and near!

Echoing Depths

In the depths where bubbles play,
Fish dance disco, bright and gay.
Anemones sway like they have the groove,
While sea stars bust a move.

Sharks are grinning, oh what a sight,
Doing the cha-cha with all their might!
Grouper's jokes make others chuckle,
While shells clink like they're in a huddle.

Down below, where the sand is soft,
Giant squids serve drinks on a loft.
With a splash and a giggle, they all align,
For an underwater party, simply divine!

Flippers slapping, and it feels so right,
Mermaids join in, ready for a bite.
In echoing depths, laughter breaks,
As each wave carries the fun it makes!

The Dance of Tides

Tides come in with a curious wave,
Tickling toes, oh how they crave!
Crabs cha-cha as the clams clap along,
The seaweed sways to a bouncy song.

Bubbles pop like jokes in the air,
While dolphins giggle without a care.
Seashells shimmer, gathering charms,
As the ocean hums its charming balms.

Sandcastles get soaked in wave-fueled fun,
And starfish roll their eyes on the run.
Join the dance, lose track of the time,
Each splash a beat in this ocean rhyme.

So grab your snorkel, join the parade,
Where sea critters jive in ocean's charade.
With every tide, new laughter is found,
In this playful dance where joy knows no bound!

Stardust and Seafoam

There once was a fish with a hat,
He danced on the waves like a brat.
He slipped on a shell,
And fell with a yell,
Rolling under a seaweed mat.

The crabs formed a band on the sand,
With rhythm that swept through the land.
They played with great glee,
But forgot the sea,
When a seagull stole their snack unplanned.

A jellyfish, quite the delight,
Wore a tutu that sparkled so bright.
She twirled with a flare,
For no one was there,
Except for a clam with a fright.

And dolphins, oh what a sight,
Practiced tricks late into the night.
But tripped on a wave,
And ended quite brave,
In a splash that gave everyone a fright.

Respite of the Shore

A crab took a sunbath, so fine,
With sunglasses and lemonade wine.
He lounged on the rock,
With a tick-tock clock,
Saying, 'Time here is simply divine.'

A seagull came down for a chat,
Said, 'You look just like a cool cat!'
But the crab just replied,
'Hey, enjoy the tide,
And stop stealing my lunch, silly brat!'

Two turtles raced fast for a snack,
But one got distracted and cracked.
He chewed on a shoe,
And then thought, 'Who knew?
That footwear could be such a whack?'

With laughter that echoed around,
Creatures danced on the warm, sandy ground.
Each wave brought a cheer,
As friends gathered near,
For fun at the shore always found.

The Depths of Solitude

In the deep where the silly fish go,
Lived a puffer who loved to steal show.
He puffed up with pride,
But then had to hide,
When he got stuck and couldn't let go.

An octopus painted his nails,
Said "This job never fails to entail,
New colors each week,
With sparkles that peek,
Yet my ink often makes funny trails."

A clam wrote a book full of lies,
About fish with the most silly ties.
But when it was read,
He turned bright red,
Because all of his facts were just cries.

In the depths, laughter rang like a bell,
With mermaids who giggled so well.
They swam bright and free,
In a world full of glee,
In a sea that had stories to tell.

Windswept Horizons

A penguin who dreamed of a flight,
Thought, 'I'll ride the wind with delight!'
He took off with style,
But stayed just a while,
Then landed with flippers all tight.

The whales held a circus at sea,
With tricks that were funny as can be.
They jumped through a hoop,
And gave each fish a scoop,
Of ice cream that rolled down a spree.

A starfish who wished for a dance,
Gave it a go without a chance.
He twirled and he spun,
With a laugh, oh what fun,
Till he slipped on a wave in a trance.

But laughter was bubbling around,
With joy that just perfectly found.
Oh, windswept delight,
With colors so bright,
In horizons where humor abounds.

Lament of the Tide Pools

In the tide pools, crabs dance,
With shells that sparkle, a funny chance.
A starfish grins, with a goofy grin,
While seaweed sways like a salty twin.

A clam's not a clam, when he jumps with glee,
Splashing water, just like a wild spree.
"Oh look at me!" says the small fish, too,
As a sea snail shows off his new tattoo.

Bubbles rise up, a popping spree,
Giggling hermit crabs, come play with me!
Tides rush in, like they're trying to race,
Who knew the sea could be such a place?

So the tide pools laugh with a jolly cheer,
In the grand sea circus, come lend an ear!
Life under waves is a comical show,
With jokes and jests that ebb to and fro.

Celestial Currents and the Great Blue

Under the stars in the deep, blue sea,
Fish tell jokes, oh so merrily!
A dolphin flips, with a wink and a twist,
While octopuses dance, you get the gist.

The sea turtles shuffle, oh what a sight!
With fins flailing left, they're a comical flight.
"Fast as a turtle!" they laugh with delight,
But really, they'll nap, and they'll do it right.

Bubbles of laughter, floating around,
Sea cucumbers crack up, without making a sound.
Whales sing out their funny old tune,
Echoing laughter beneath the moon.

So sail through the night, let your worries slip,
With friends in the sea, take a giddy trip.
Celestial currents will carry your jest,
In depths of the blue, you'll find the best.

Reflections in the Surging Surf

Waves winking back, a cheeky sight,
Tide rolls in, then takes its flight.
A seagull squawks, with a silly call,
As shells tumble down, like a giant ball.

The surf brings secrets, it whispers and plays,
Time for shenanigans, oh what a craze!
Fish jump high, wearing shades so bright,
In the splash of the waves, they dance with delight.

"Surf's up!" they laugh, in a watery rush,
With sea foam giggles, they form quite a hush.
A crab on a board sought the perfect wave,
Sailing past shells, oh, how they misbehave!

So ride on the crests, let joy overflow,
In the swell of the surf, let the laughter grow.
With each rolling wave, find a reason to cheer,
Reflections of fun always bring us near.

Forgotten Shores and Lost Tales

On forgotten shores, where the driftwood lies,
Mermaids gossip under calm skies.
"Did you hear that wave is a great singer?"
With their scales shimmering, their giggles linger.

A pirate's hat floats; where's the captain now?
With seagulls debating, "No, not here, wow!"
The treasure is laughter, tucked in the sand,
Where crabs tell the tales of their silly band.

Old tales get lost, as the tide rolls away,
Whispers of fish, in a playful display.
"Can you believe that shark? He tried to dance!"
Yet stumbled on kelp—it was quite a chance!

So stroll on the beach, let the laughter fly,
On shores that forget, as the waves sigh.
In shimmering sands, find the joy that prevails,
In forgotten stories, where humor never fails.

The Language of Waves

The waves crash down with quite a sound,
    Like fishy whispers circling 'round.
They gurgle secrets, tales so grand,
    But I just wish they'd lend a hand.

They slap the shore and run away,
    Like kids refusing games to play.
I shout at them to come back near,
    But all I get is salty cheer!

They tumble high and dance with glee,
    With crabby dancers, wild and free.
I wave my arms, and laugh aloud,
    At nature's quirky, splashy crowd.

So next time waves come rolling by,
    Just grab a shell, and say hi!
But be prepared, they'll surely tease,
    With salty jokes carried on the breeze.

Transience of the Breeze

The breeze comes in with a cheeky grin,
It tickles my nose, then takes a spin.
It swirls around, it's never still,
A playful rascal, a wind-up thrill.

One moment here, the next it's gone,
It plays hide and seek from dusk till dawn.
With a whoosh and a giggle, it sweeps the sand,
Leaving footprints from its invisible hand.

It whispers jokes, it rustles leaves,
Conspiracies that no one believes.
But oh, that breeze, such a crafty sly,
It bumps my hat and makes me cry!

So when it comes with breezy flare,
Just laugh along, dance in the air.
For every gust that sweeps your way,
Is just good fun on a windy day!

Colors of the Coral

Oh coral reefs, you're quite a sight,
In colors bold, you're pure delight.
Pink, blue, yellow, and a touch of green,
A coral party, the most vibrant scene!

The fish swim by in formal wear,
With fins that flutter, oh so rare!
They gossip about the seaweed's style,
And sneak in jokes that make me smile.

Anemones wave like they own the place,
With tentacles dancing, such grace and pace!
They tickle the fish, make them jump and dart,
Nature's funny artwork, a true sea chart.

So when you dive in those colors bright,
Remember to laugh, it feels so right.
For in this carnival under the sea,
The colors of coral bring glee, oh me!

Light Beneath the Crest

The crests rise up in a foamy dance,
Catching sunlight in a bubbly trance.
They sparkle like diamonds, oh what a show,
But watch your head, here comes a big blow!

Below the waves, it's a circus scene,
With playful dolphins, bright and keen.
They leap through light, like giggling sprites,
Turning the sea into dazzling sights.

The shadows try to throw a prank,
But the fish just laugh, and swim with thank.
For every splash, there's laughter in tow,
As nature's crew steals the show.

So if you happen to catch that light,
Join in the giggles, it feels just right.
Under the crest, where joy is found,
The sea's a stage, and fun knows no bound!

Currents of Calm and Chaos

Waves crash and tumble with glee,
Spraying my sandwich, oh, woe is me!
The seaweed dances, a slimy ballet,
Laughing at swimmers who belly-flop play.

Fish in tuxedos, the ocean's own show,
Throwing confetti as bubbles do blow.
Laughter erupts when a seal makes a noise,
Guests on the shore bring their boisterous joys.

Jellyfish jiggle like blobs in the blue,
While crabs sneak a peek, oh how rude of you!
Chaos awaits on this sandy expanse,
With each splash and giggle, we all take a chance.

Lighthouses and Shadows

A lighthouse stands tall, but it winks,
Making the seagulls question their shrinks.
Casting a glow in the dead of the night,
With shadows that dance, oh what a sight!

Nautical ghosts doing the cha-cha,
Boo. Did I scare you? Haha, hurrah!
The waves they tickle the rocks as they dash,
While sailors believe it's a friendly splash.

Beach balls float by, like ships full of glee,
As shadows put on a wild jamboree.
The beacon just chuckles, in its own quirky way,
Inviting the night in for a comical play.

Embracing the Abyss

Diving down deep where the weird fish dwell,
They throw a party, oh can you tell?
With googly eyes and a dance so bizarre,
They're the ocean's weirdos, like rock stars from afar.

A sunken ship told me a joke or two,
When the crabs did the conga, it was oddly true.
A chorus of clams sang in perfect off-key,
We laughed till we floated, oh what a spree!

Octopuses clapping with eight-pointed grace,
While turtles did slow-motion in a weird race.
The abyss isn't scary, just full of surprises,
With creatures that giggle in odd, funny disguises.

Sonnet to Seagulls

Oh seagulls, you rascals, so bold and so free,
With your raucous caws, a comedy spree.
You steal my chips with a quick, crafty dive,
Then squawk to your friends: "Look how I thrive!"

On piers you gather like comedians' role,
Claiming the sandwiches, that's your main goal.
You strut on the sands, like royalty proud,
While sunbathers shout, "Hey! That's not allowed!"

But we laugh along with your mischief-filled flight,
Chasing the waves, a hilarious sight.
Oh seagulls, dear jesters of skies and shore,
Your antics make us smile forevermore.

Secrets in the Seashell

I found a shell, thought it was grand,
Said it held secrets from a far-off land.
But when I held it up to my ear,
All I heard was my neighbor's sneer.

I tried to listen for mermaid's tunes,
But all I got was the sound of typhoons.
I wondered if fish tell jokes and sing,
Or just sit around and do their fishy thing.

I wanted wisdom from waves and foam,
But learned instead about seaweed's comb.
The crabs are grumpy, the seagulls rude,
Sea secrets are often a real damp mood!

So if you find a shell on the shore,
Know it may gossip, but it won't keep score.
She's a spy, a chatter, but when push comes to shove,
She's really just a big ol' saltwater glove.

Driftwood Memories

I saw some driftwood, thought it was neat,
Wrote a whole saga with a twist of a beat.
But it turned out to be a toilet seat,
Nature sure has a quirky suite!

Wooden logs thinking they're part of the crew,
Claiming they're wooden whales, but they really just stew.

I built a castle, but it fell in a flash,
Turns out the tide hates a clumsy splash.

Let's crown the driftwood as king of the shore,
For its life has a twist, oh, what a bore!
It ships off to sunsets, then bounces away,
Probably off to a seaside cabaret.

In my head, driftwood dances and spins,
While telling the tales of sea monster sins.
But the truth is, it's just taking a nap,
While I bum on the beach, dreaming of a map!

Whispers of the Tide

The tide came in with a giggle today,
It tickled my toes and danced on my stray.
I swear it whispered, 'Come join the fun!'
But when I dived in, it just made me run!

Seagulls were laughing, flipping their wings,
At silly humans chasing sea slings.
They squawked out warnings, oh my, oh wow!
But I thought they were cheering, not taking a bow!

I built a grand sandcastle, tall as could be,
But the tide had plans, a real sneaky spree.
Just when I thought I was queen of the beach,
It took my whole castle—such a sneaky breach!

But the ocean's chuckle was hard to resist,
With waves that wiggle like they can't be missed.
So I'll dance with the tide, no need to abide,
I'll just laugh with the sea, let the waves be my guide!

Freedom of the Open Waters

I set sail with joy, on the wild, wide sea,
My boat started wobbling, was it just me?
With waves bouncing high, and clouds made of fluff,
I realized quickly, I'm just not that tough!

A fish jumped aboard, said, 'What's the rush?'
'Calm down, silly, or you'll cause quite the fuss!'
I replied, 'Mr. Fish, I'm looking for fun!'
He simply laughed, 'It's better when you're done.'

The sea breeze was friendly, like a warm pat,
But the sunburn that followed? No thanks, I'm fat!
I danced with the dolphins, twirled with a crab,
Made friends with the seaweed—it gave me a gab!

But tides turned stern, whispers turned loud,
While I cozied up, looking quite proud.
A seagull swooped down, took my sandwich with glee,
I guess freedom's fun, but watch out for that spree!

Gypsy Waves

Waves are quite the jokers, you see,
They tickle your toes and dance with glee.
One tries to trip you, while others retreat,
Making sandcastles flop, but oh, what a treat!

Seagulls laugh loud as they swoop for a fry,
Whispering secrets as they dash by.
They steal all your chips, then carry away,
Leaving salty reminders of a fun-filled day!

Crabs do a conga upon the wet sand,
Clicking their claws, looking quite grand.
Shells play the drums in a sandy parade,
Everywhere you go, there's a show to invade!

So grab your floatie and join in the fun,
With slippery slides and a splash in the sun.
Life by the water's a giggle and cheer,
Letting waves wash away all of your fear.

Sheltered by the Sea

Under the water, so snug and warm,
Fish throw parties, it's quite the swarm.
With bubbles like confetti, they dance and they spin,
Dressed in bright colors, where to begin?

Starfish are lounge chairs, relaxing with style,
Collecting sunbeams, they've been there awhile.
Seashells gossip like wise old folks,
In the shade of a wave, they share silly jokes!

The tide brings surprises, be ready to cheer,
A shoe or a beach ball could suddenly appear!
Crabs masquerade, thinking they're quite neat,
Wearing silly hats, tap dancing on feet.

So if you are weary, just dive in and play,
The sea's full of laughter to brighten your day.
With friends all around in this watery realm,
Joy is the captain, you're at the helm!

Whispers Among the Corals

Corals chat softly, while fish tell a tale,
Of lost flip-flops and jellyfish trails.
They giggle and wiggle in colors so bright,
Creating a scene, a dazzling sight!

Anemones wave like they're in a parade,
Tickling the fish as they frolic and fade.
A sea cucumber trips, what a sight to behold!
With laughter erupting from creatures bold.

Turtles glide gently, with wisdom so deep,
They nod at the sea urchins, who silently creep.
"Oh, the joys of the ocean!" a clam declares loud,
"I've got a pearl," he says, "wasn't it proud?"

Among the corals, the merriment grows,
As bubbles rise up, and everyone knows.
Life's a grand dance in the tidal embrace,
Where humor and joy are the truest grace.

Dance Partners of the Wind and Water

The wind spins and twirls, it whispers and sings,
Breezing through palm trees, happy with springs.
Water joins in with its splashy reply,
Together they play, oh my, how they fly!

Dolphins are acrobats, leaping with cheer,
They invite the gulls to join them here.
A waltz with the waves, a shimmy in blue,
What a fantastic dance party, just for you!

The sun joins the party, beaming so bright,
Casting sparkles that twinkle and light.
Shells clap along to the rhythm so grand,
As creatures of the sea form a jubilant band.

So come, dip your toes and sway with delight,
In nature's own ballet, from morning to night.
In this joyful ballet of water and air,
You'll find there's no party as fun, we declare!

Chasing Horizons and Echoes

Seagulls squawk like clowns, it's true,
I wave at them like they wave back too.
Sunburned noses, all shades of red,
Who thought sunscreen was just for the head?

As I chase horizons, my hat takes flight,
It sails like a ship in the broad daylight.
My friends just laugh, they're stuck in their seats,
Chasing horizons and dodging my feats!

Crabs dance sideways like they own the shore,
I join their ballet, but they ask for more.
With wobbly legs and a tip-top grin,
Even the fish are just waiting to win.

So here's to the waves and the towel fights,
Splashing my friends in the summer nights.
We're silly and lost, caught in the flow,
Chasing echoes where wild antics grow.

Crystals of the Coral Veil

Beneath the waves, where fish like to play,
Zebras swim by in their fancy ballet.
"Quick, take a picture!" I holler with glee,
But it's a blurry selfie with a seaweed tree.

The coral looks cheap, like a plastic surprise,
I poke it softly, and it gives me the eyes.
"Stop prodding me, buddy, I'm not your toy,
I'm worth way more than that, oh boy, oh boy!"

Clams snap at laughter, crabs click in cheer,
They're having a party, I think I'll join here.
Who knew underwater could be such a treat?
Dancing and laughing with fish on repeat!

So let's toast to the shells, champagne of the sea,
With flavors of salt, and a hint of brie.
Under the water, our worries dissolve,
In a world full of laughter, we all evolve.

Beyond the Whispering Waves

I dip my toes in the shimmer and shine,
Fish tease my ankles and consider it fine.
With every splash, they seem to conspire,
Plotting some nonsense as I start to tire.

A dolphin pops up, says, "Wanna race?"
I trip on my flip-flops, fall flat on my face.
He laughs with delight, and I groan with pain,
Guess I'll just stick to my sandcastle reign.

Waves whisper secrets, soft tales in the night,
Seagulls throw shade like they're born for the fight.
I read them a story about fish in disguise,
They squawk and they flail, what a world full of lies!

So let's skip the worries, take a dive for a laugh,
And mingle with seaweed, our nature's gaffe.
In this wacky water, where nonsense flows,
Beyond quiet whispers, our fun only grows.

The Heartbeat of the Abyss

Down in the deep, where the shadows get thick,
I'm dodging a jellyfish, a true nasty trick.
They pulse like disco lights, what a silly sight,
I try to dance back, but they're just too bright.

The octopus laughs, says, "Come join my game!"
I'm tangled and whipped, it's a wild, silly fame.
With ink sprays and giggles, I'm lost in the mire,
Thought I was cool, now I'm stuck in their fire!

Claims boast their pearls, like they're all in the know,
But I'm just here tripping on seaweed in tow.
A clam turns its shell, "You think you're so grand?"
As I wipe off the sand from the mess on my hand.

So cheers to the depths, where the strange things reside,
With laughter and bubbles, it's quite the wild ride.
In the heartbeat below, our spirits unwind,
Making memories so funny, you'll never mind.

Soft Serenity of the Swells

Waves giggle and splash, making a scene,
Crabs dance around like they've lost their sheen.
Seagulls swoop low, stealing my fries,
While fish play tag, in silly disguise.

Sandcastles topple, the tide's a prankster,
Shells hide treasures that smell like a gangster.
Jellyfish float, doing a wiggly jive,
While I try to swim, just hoping to survive.

The sun wears shades, it's a silly sight,
As dolphins mimic, "Hey, dude, hold tight!"
Splashing about, just having a laugh,
Even the seaweed's got a photo staff.

With laughter and fun, and a splash of glee,
This watery world just tickles me!
In every wiggle, in every wave,
Who knew the sea could be so brave?

Breeze Between the Rocks

Winds whisper secrets, tickling my nose,
As sea turtles giggle in their graceful clothes.
A puff of salt air, a sneeze I can't hold,
This playful breeze makes my stories unfold.

Barnacles gossip, perched on their throne,
"Don't you judge us, we're more than just bone!"
The sea cucumbers roll, in a jelly-like spree,
Starmaps in sand, not a single degree.

Lobsters have parties, but dance like a plank,
Playing limbo 'neath the kelp forest tank.
Octopi juggle, just trying to show,
That underwater antics are the way to go!

In the breeze's embrace, I laugh and I sway,
In this zany world where I'd love to play.
So let's ride the waves, under the bright sun,
Fishy frolics are truly just fun!

Guardians of the Shallows

Crabs in their armor, they march with flair,
"Watch out!" they click, "We're kings of the dare!"
Starfish lounge, too lazy to move,
While minnows swarm in a curious groove.

Seashells tell tales of pirates and loot,
"Finders keepers," they cry, "Isn't it cute?"
The mantis shrimp flexes its colorful shell,
With moves so sharp, it might just rebel.

Eels peek out, with a glance of disdain,
"Who needs a crown when you can have a mane?"
With bubble-blowing fish and turtle charm,
The shallows are safe, there's no need for alarm!

So here in this realm, where silliness swims,
Every tale told is a giggly whim.
With guardians who skip, and tales full of cheer,
Dive into this laughter, let's all persevere!

Merging with the Mist

Fog rolls in slow, draping the coast,
"Boo!" whispers a wave, like a playful ghost.
With laughter that lingers, the mist likes to tease,
As sea urchins chuckle, hidden beneath leaves.

The horizon giggles, tickling the sky,
"With every high tide, we'll watch you fly!"
A sea otter lounges, on a drifting vine,
"Life's too short for seriousness, just pass the brine!"

Splashing and crashing, the surf comes to play,
While dolphins encourage, "Come join the fray!"
We tumble through bubbles, and flip with a cheer,
This misty mild world is far from austere.

So let's twirl with joy, in this foggy delight,
Where silliness swims, and the laughter feels right.
Each wave whispers fun, as we merge and unwind,
In this swirling joy, silly stories we'll find!

Colors of Dusk on the Waves

The sun dips low, a cheeky prank,
Splashing pinks on the sky's big tank.
Seagulls laugh, they swoop and dive,
Playing tag, oh, how they thrive!

Flip-flops flop and the kids all squeal,
Chasing crabs, what a perfect deal!
A jellyfish floats, doing the twist,
"Hey, don't touch me!" it seems to insist.

Sandcastles crumble, oh what a shame,
'Twas a grand fortress, now just a game.
A tide rolls in with a sneaky smile,
"Not today!" it shouts, "Just wait a while!"

With giggles and splashes, we jump in the foam,
This watery world feels just like home.
As colors dance and the laughter sways,
We wave goodbye to our silly days.

Guardians of the Shoreline

On sandy thrones, the crabs do sway,
In tiny armor, they keep woes at bay.
Dressed in shells like kings, they strut,
"Watch your toes!" they warn, "Or you'll feel a cut!"

An octopus dons a pince-nez so neat,
Evaluating swimmers from its cozy seat.
"Not today, my friend, that's a big splash!"
It winks a tentacle, then makes a dash!

Seagulls squawk their royal decree,
"Treats for the brave, but watch for the brie!"
They swoop and glide, jesters of the skies,
Taking bread rolls and chips as their prize.

The tide rolls back, a cheeky retreat,
Leaving behind a salty treat.
The guardians laugh, another day spent,
In a realm where laughter and sand are rent.

Tales from the Abyss

Beneath the waves, where the seaweed flops,
A mermaid's caught in a game of hop.
She's tangled in kelp, oh what a sight,
Flipping her tail, she's ready to fight!

Fish with sunglasses swim by with flair,
"Did you see that?" they announce with a stare.
A dolphin's giggle rings bright as a bell,
"Who's up for a race? Bet I swim well!"

The squid tells tales of the great big blue,
"Once I saw a ship, and its crew, oh so true!
They tossed me a snack, but I squirted ink,
Now they tell stories, make you think!"

Anemones wave, giving hugs so snug,
While eels play tease, just to give a shrug.
Undersea laughter echoes amidst the cheer,
In this deep, silly place, it's always clear!

The Unfurling Current

Here comes the tide, with a sneaky grin,
Pushing driftwood, letting the fun begin.
A beach ball bounces, a dance in the spray,
"Catch me if you can!" it seems to say.

Kids in their goggles, a floatie parade,
Marching to conquer waves unafraid!
An inflatable shark, "I'm the king!"
"Not in my pool!" cries a dolphin with bling.

With boogie boards flying, the laughter erupts,
Planks and splashes, oh how they erupt!
Sandwiches fly, and sunscreen too,
Who knew the current loved snacks that blue?

The sun sets slow, a playful bow,
As we gather our treasures, take a final vow.
Tomorrow we'll come, with giggles once more,
To where the currents dance on the shore!

Currents of Silence

Waves giggle as they dance around,
They're playing tag without a sound.
Seagulls squawk with silly flair,
While crabs in shells pretend to care.

Starfish plotting on the sand,
Making castles, oh so grand.
Fish in masks swim by with grace,
While clams play cards in their own space.

Turtles wearing shades, so cool,
Ride the tides like it's a pool.
Jellyfish bounce, a trampoline,
In an underwater dream machine.

Then the tide pulls back to shore,
And seaweed dances, craving more.
The sun dips low, the sea's awake,
With giggles hidden in each wave's break.

Salty Kisses at Dusk

The sun winks as it starts to dip,
Waves make bubbles, they're on a trip.
Sandcastles topple, laughter flows,
As starfish wear their little bows.

Crabs do the cha-cha on the line,
A shellfish party, feeling fine.
Seashells gossip, tales so grand,
While octopuses take the band.

The evening tide brings light and cheer,
With plankton stars that twinkle near.
Sea cucumbers dance with zest,
While fish flash smiles, they're the best.

As night unfolds, the ocean sighs,
With starlit dreams beneath the skies.
A salty breeze, the moon's sweet kiss,
In a world of waves, we find our bliss.

Echoes Beneath the Surface

Bubbles giggle, secrets swell,
Echoes bubble like a tale to tell.
Mermaids swap their hair-braiding tips,
While dolphins sing and do backflips.

The fish chatter in colors bright,
Playing tag in the fading light.
Coral reefs spark laughter's tease,
As turtles chase the dancing breeze.

Bold barnacles with swagger strut,
On the rocks, they waddle but.
Sea horses play poker with shells,
While clam shells hold their laughing spells.

In the twilight, the water glows,
With giggles drifting where the current flows.
A symphony of waves and fun,
Under a blanket of stars, all spun.

Nautical Reverie

Sailboats waltz on a breezy trail,
While fish throw parties without fail.
Lobsters in tuxes dance the night,
While plankton twirl in sheer delight.

A buoy becomes a disco ball,
As seagulls dive and take a fall.
Starfish rock out, a gentle sway,
In the salty spray, they play all day.

The captain's hat, a seagull claim,
Chasing shoals of tiny fame.
Barnacles cheer from the sidelines wide,
With a chortle that won't subside.

In this realm where laughter thrives,
All manner of surprise arrives.
As waves crash down, the joy's dispersed,
In a nautical world where fun is first!

Serenades of Sailors

Upon the waves, a sailor sings,
His fishy tales of grand old things.
With seagulls cackling, pulling pranks,
They steal his hat, oh how he tanks!

His shipmates laugh, they toss some fries,
While fish swim by, with bulging eyes.
They jive with mermaids, dance and spin,
Till one gets caught in a sailor's grin.

With barrels rolling, laughter flies,
Each salty breeze is filled with sighs.
They tip their cups, the sea's their muse,
A dolphin dives, then steals a snooze!

So here's to sailors, brave and bold,
With stories funny, never old.
They sail the seas with banter free,
And chase the tides, like a bumblebee!

Fragile Ecosystems

In coral castles, fish do prance,
With clumsy crabs who try to dance.
They bump and bruise like silly fools,
While seaweed waves, as if in schools.

An octopus, with inked-up flair,
Casts shadow puppets in mid-air.
The starfish sit, pretending wise,
As barnacles plot their crafty lies.

A clam sings low, a shellfish tune,
While shrimp hold court under the moon.
A jellyfish floats, with fashion bright,
His random jabs create pure fright!

Yet in this chaos, life persists,
With giggles shared, and playful twists.
So here's a toast to this fine crew,
To fragile friends beneath the blue!

Treasures Lost in the Brine

Beneath the waves, a shoe, once fine,
Now rusted treasures in the brine.
A pirate's tooth, a coin or two,
And Betty's glasses, pink and blue!

A teddy bear, once loved, now lost,
While coral reefs, at buoyed cost,
They hide their finds with salty glee,
For treasure maps were drawn by sea!

A sock that lost its partner bold,
A bottle with messages untold.
And whispers of a shipwrecked eye,
With tales of snacks that went awry!

Yet with each dive, a giggle forms,
As flotsam dances through the storms.
What's lost may find its way to shore,
In tales of treasure, evermore!

Mysterious Depths

In deep blue realms where shadows play,
Strange creatures hide, away from day.
With grinning sharks and clown fish too,
The deep sea holds a comedy crew!

An anglerfish, with light so bright,
Says, "Come here and see my fright!"
While others giggle in the gloom,
They've turned his bait into a broom!

A sea turtle dons a fancy hat,
While jellyfish sway, like they're at bat.
The deep sea's ball, it's quite the sight,
Where laughter echoes through the night!

So raise your fins, let's give a cheer,
For creatures funny, far and near.
In depths of blue, where humor reigns,
Adventure waits through watery lanes!

Reflections of a Nautical Dream

A fish in a suit, oh what a sight,
Looking for a job, from morning till night.
He searches for treasure, but finds only pearls,
Dancing with crabs, and doing some twirls.

Seagulls do gossip in the salty breeze,
Complaining about seamen, and their old knees.
While octopuses juggle with lost fishing lines,
The dolphin's the judge, with a helmet of vines.

A turtle on a surfboard, what a fun ride,
Declares he'll travel across the wide tide.
But with every wave, he's tossed to and fro,
Screaming, "I should've stayed back in my show!"

Bubbles are laughter, floating so high,
Betting on whales who can leap to the sky.
With mackerel jokes that tickle the sand,
We're all just a splash in this whimsical land.

Deep Calls to Deep

Beneath the surface, a crab plays a tune,
He thinks he's a rockstar, singing to the moon.
But every time he strums with his claw,
He gets tangled in seaweed, oh what a flaw!

A lobster in shades, sunbathing with pride,
Says, "I'm too cool to be caught, I'll just hide!"
Yet the fisherman chuckles, his net in the air,
"Good luck with your tan, you're in for a scare!"

The eel tells tall tales, a slippery sort,
About treasure and pirates, a grand old retort.
But when he gets caught in a fisherman's net,
He whines, "I was just rehearsing, don't be upset!"

Starfish with five wishes, makes quite a fuss,
But wishes for pizza cause quite a disgust.
Yet the sea laughs along, it's quirky and wild,
In this world full of giggles, it's always beguiled.

Shadows Beneath the Blue

Down in the depths, where shadows do play,
A flounder in costume, sways all day.
With a hat made of kelp, he's quite the sensation,
He's off to the ball, in a fishy formation.

Tropical fish gossip, they flutter and spin,
"Who wore it better, that clownfish or twin?"
Water's too warm for a heated debate,
They settle their scores over seaweed on plates.

A shark tries to dance, with two left fins,
Crashing through corals, apologetic grins.
He asks for a lesson, bright dolphins oblige,
"Just don't eat your partners, it's quite the surprise!"

Medusa makes jelly, with squid as the chef,
"I'm trendy!" she yells, "Many will envy my rep!"
But when it's all done, the big fish all sigh,
"Our diets can't handle this wave of a fry!"

Clarity in Ocean Depths

In crystal-clear waters, a clam starts to mime,
Pretending to be a great poet of rhyme.
He writes with his tongue, a real wordsmith's loot,
Though readers prefer tales from the dapper old brute.

A pufferfish ponder, with thoughts that are grand,
"Nobody respects me, just look at the band!"
The clownfish just giggles, "You're trying too hard,
Just be yourself, it's not that avant-garde!"

Jellyfish shuffle, with dances so free,
Their moves make the seaweed sway with glee.
While anemones stand, with arms crossed in awe,
Critiquing their rhythm, in a floral faux pas!

With a sea cucumber's wisdom, and laughter so bright,
Life in the depths is a whimsical sight.
So raise up a fin, and enjoy the deep jest,
For humor as vast, will always be best!

Sirens' Songs and Sandy Footprints

On sandy beaches, crabs give chase,
Seagulls dive with charming grace.
A mermaid's laughter fills the air,
With frothy hair and fishy flair.

Shells wear hats, a silly sight,
As dolphins dance in pure delight.
They whisper tales of treasure found,
In fishy voices, joyous sound.

The starfish play a game of tag,
While jellyfish float in the lag.
A seaweed wig on a fishy dude,
In a watery world, we're never rude.

So join me here where fun's the goal,
On waves that crash and bubbles roll.
We'll swirl and twirl, just like a whirl,
And laugh with mermaids, oh what a pearl!

Mosaic of the Deep

Beneath the waves, a clownfish grins,
With playful puns, he surely wins.
Corals bloom in colors bright,
While octopuses rock out all night.

Sea turtles sport a silly look,
With shells designed from storybooks.
They paddle slowly, oh so sly,
While crabs compete in races nearby.

A blowfish puffs, then shrieks with glee,
"Who's got the biggest fish, not me!"
Barbarians of the briny blue,
Create a splash, a hullabaloo.

Amongst the bubbles, laughter rings,
With every flip, the ocean sings.
So take a dip and join the fun,
In this mosaic, life has begun!

Windswept Wishes on the Shoreline

A seagull squawks, "Hey, watch my dive!"
As beach balls bounce and sea folks thrive.
The sandcastles rise, but oh what a sight,
When waves come crashing, they take flight!

With windswept wishes, we cast our dreams,
While kids giggle and ice cream streams.
Sandy feet run, slip, and slide,
While sand crabs scuttle full of pride.

A flip flop flies amidst the cheer,
As sunscreen battles with salty beer.
The shore is alive with giggles and glee,
While tanned tourists shout, "Look at me!"

So grab your friends, let's build a fort,
Where laughter echoes, and waves cavort.
We'll dance and jump 'til the stars appear,
In this windswept realm of fun we cheer!

Unfurling Vows of the Sea

Two fish say 'I do' in bubbles bright,
With seashell rings and hearts of light.
Their wedding's grand, no heart to lack,
As dolphins flip, they won't hold back.

The vows are made with salty kisses,
In waning tides, no room for misses.
With jellybeans and kelp bouquet,
This wedding's a splashy, funny display!

The crabs all dance, a jolly crew,
In tuxedos of sand, oh what a view!
With fishy friends, they celebrate,
As barnacles cheer, "It's never too late!"

From twirling currents to the sunny spree,
They vow to be happy, wild, and free.
So step right up, join in the fun,
These vows unfurl, two hearts become one!

Moonlit Ripples and Secrets

Beneath the moon, waves play tag,
They giggle and dance, with a splash and a brag.
Secrets are whispered by the blue,
Even the fish yawn, 'What a hullabaloo!'

Stars twinkle down, joining the fun,
As jellyfish glide, a soft, glowing run.
Crabs do the moonwalk, oh what a sight,
While seaweed sways, in the soft, silver light.

Gulls in Flight

Over the waves, gulls flap and squawk,
Chasing their tails, like they own the dock.
They steal a fry, then play the fool,
Calling each other, 'Hey, that was cool!'

A beak here, a wing there, a flurry of flair,
These feathered rascals, without a care.
Wheeling and dealing in the salty breeze,
They dive-bomb snacks with the greatest of ease.

Cormorants Dive

Cormorants dive with style and grace,
Plunging below, it's a watery race.
They pop up with fish, looking quite sly,
And flash a big smile, oh me, oh my!

With a flap and a flick, they aim for the shore,
Chasing each other, this game they adore.
But fish are quick, they wiggle and flee,
Leaving the birds in a splashy decree!

Celestial Driftwood

Driftwood floats, thinking it's a boat,
While crabs hold a meeting, dressed up in coat.
They chat about tides, and what's on the menu,
Planning a feast, with sea lettuce to chew!

A starfish arrives, all glitter and cheer,
With eight fancy arms, it's the place to be near.
"Let's throw a dance," it shouts with delight,
While driftwood believes it might take flight!

Tide's Embrace at Twilight

As twilight falls, and the tide gives a wink,
The sand giggles, ready for a drink.
Seashells gossip, swapping old tales,
Of mermaids' parties and spouting whale trails.

The waves tinker gently, like kids with a kite,
While barnacles rock out, to the rhythm of night.
Under the sky, the creatures take flight,
In this silly, sandy, twilight delight!

Beneath the Blue Canopy

Bubbles rise, a fishy sneeze,
Jellyfish float with such great ease.
Seagulls squawk, a feathery choir,
Wonder who steals the fisherman's fryer?

Crabs do a dance, it's quite a sight,
Pinching toes just feels so right.
Starfish giggle, stars in disguise,
Playing hide and seek in their sunny ties.

Turtles surf on waves so high,
While clams prefer to sit and sigh.
Oceanweed sways like a funky band,
Dancing to beats from the sandy land.

Octopus jokes, tell me a pun!
"Why did the fish join the swim run?
To catch a wave and make a splash!"
Beneath the blue, life's a funny bash!

Sirens in the Deep

Mermaids laugh in a bubbling spree,
Flipping tails, full of glee.
"Why did the sailor break up with me?"
"Too much baggage in his fishy sea!"

They croon sweet songs to lure and tease,
While fish roll eyes, just do as they please.
One mermaid lost her golden comb,
"Anyone seen it near my foamy home?"

The crabs all chuckle, shifting their gear,
"I found it once, but now I fear,
It's stuck in seaweed, a tangled mess,
Who knew hairstyles could cause such distress?"

Echoes of laughter leap through the tide,
As each wave carries tales far and wide.
Neptune shakes his head, a grin on his face,
In the depths of the sea, there's always a place!

Horizon's Embrace

Underneath skies of the bluest hue,
Seagulls coordinate a seafood crew.
"Who needs a ship when a plank will do?"
Life's a deck party, with waves to pursue!

Fishing lines tangled, a sight to behold,
Fishermen grumble, but they're mostly bold.
"You caught my hat, that's no fishing tale,
Now it's swimming home, riding the gale."

Pelicans dive in, necks on parade,
While dolphins jump and dance in cascade.
"Catch me a snack!" one dolphin declares,
And a crab responds, "Not in these layers!"

The sunset paints laughter on waves all around,
As fish swap jokes in a comedic sound.
A banquet of humor, a feast for the heart,
Adventures afloat, let the fun times start!

Serenade of Stormy Seas

Up above, the clouds form a frown,
Waves roll high, trying to take the crown.
A pirate ship shouts, "Can I get a drink?"
As rain pours down, they swim and sink.

Mermaids hold umbrellas, quite the scene,
While thunder grumbles, "That's too routine!"
"Hold onto your hats!" a sailor cries brave,
As the wind gives a laugh—an oceanic wave.

The shrimps throw a party in spite of the storm,
While sea cucumbers try to keep warm.
"Why are we stuck here?" a clam starts to pout,
"Because you won't share your snack!" comes the shout!

So here's to the storms where laughter is brewed,
Where every wave comes with a comical mood.
Life's unpredictable, a funny ol' ride,
In the serenade where humor must abide!

A Canvas of Aquatic Shadows

Bubbles rise, fish wear hats,
Octopuses juggle, imagine that!
A crab with glasses reads a book,
As seaweed dancers give a look.

Turtles skate on sandy floors,
Seagulls sing of ocean shores.
The waves are giggling, can't you hear?
Anemones chuckle, full of cheer.

Starfish are dreaming by the waves,
Casting wishes, oh so brave!
Mermaids play hide and seek, you see,
While the fish swim round the coral tree.

Shells are gossiping, all in tune,
Crabs recite poems while the fish croon.
Underwater parties, what a sight,
The sea's a circus, day or night!

Dancing with the Water Spirits

Flip-flops lost, who needs those?
While mermaids flaunt, a fishy pose!
Dolphins twirl in synchronized spree,
   Waving tails, quite fancy-free.

Jellyfish disco, feet in the air,
With knee-slapping moves, they dance without care.
The sea cucumbers join in too,
   Making memories in shades of blue.

Sandy toes tap to sea's own beat,
A crab conductor, oh so neat!
The tide's a rhythm, keen and quick,
Everyone's grooving, no one's a stick!

With giggles and splashes, they whirl around,
Ocean's laughter, in waves profound.
Who knew the deep could be so bright?
Beneath the surface, pure delight!

Secrets of the Salted Horizon

The tide tells tales of seashells lost,
A fish with dreams, but what's the cost?
Nudging waves, they whisper low,
About the treasures the currents flow.

Barnacles grumble in secret unions,
While crabs team up for a wild reunion.
The starfish complain, "We're stuck, oh dear!"
Laughing bubbles, never fear!

Seagulls plot a sneaky scheme,
To snatch a snack, or so it seems.
With beaks like hooks, they grab and go,
Smart pelicans struggle, moving slow.

Among the rocks, secrets conspire,
Dancing currents spark their fire.
The salty crew, with charms galore,
Makes life in the depths never a bore!

A Voyage Through Blue Remembrance

Sailing logs with dreams afloat,
Whales pass by, they take note!
A captain fish with shell back hat,
Commands the crew of crabs so sprat.

With sea breeze tickling their fins,
They laugh at stories, old, not thin.
The gear is silly, mismatched in size,
Flippers squeaking, oh what a surprise!

They chart a course with jelly pen,
Navigating laughter, again and again.
Stars shining bright, but all's not well,
The sea monsters tease, with a playful yell!

Yet every wave brings smiles anew,
On this epic voyage, through and through.
With memories cast in ocean's play,
Life is a party, come what may!

Dance of the Algae

Algae in green, doing a jig,
Wiggling and wobbling, looking quite big.
They twirl and they spin, a slippery sight,
Making fish giggle with all of their might.

The crabs join the party, a dance on the sand,
With moves so absurd, it's totally unplanned.
They shuffle and shuffle, in rhythm they glide,
All while the seagulls just watch, open-eyed.

A dolphin drops in, trying to impress,
With flips and with flops, causing a mess.
Fish roll on the floor, laughing their fins,
As algae keep dancing, it's where fun begins.

But suddenly a wave crashes the bash,
With a swoosh and a splash, it cleared the whole stash.
They'll grumble and moan, await the next tide,
In hopes for a flow where laughter can bide.

Moonlit Water's Lullaby

A fish with a hat croons a soft tune,
Under the glow of a silvery moon.
The stars tap their fins, keeping the beat,
As turtles all dance with flippers and feet.

A crab plays the spoons, what a strange sound,
While seals do the cha-cha, spinning around.
With bubbles for notes and seaweed for flair,
They whirl in the night with nary a care.

But a jellyfish floats, feeling quite blue,
Saying, "Where's my invite, I want to groove too!"
The octopus shrugs with a wink and a grin,
"Join us, dear friend, let the fun now begin!"

As laughter erupts, the moon shines down bright,
Lighting the waves for this comical night.
In the watery depths, where joy's found anew,
Each creature rejoices, as life's just a brew.

A Symphony of Shells

Shells gather around, for a concert tonight,
With clams playing drums, oh what a delight!
Oysters on violins, quite fancy and proud,
While snails are the trumpets, wailing out loud.

The conch leads the way, with a big bold blast,
Saying, "Let's jam out, we're having a blast!"
Waves enhance the rhythm, a natural beat,
As every shell creature finds it hard to seat.

But wait! What's that? It's a clam gone rogue,
Bouncing about like a bead on a log!
Cracking a joke, he cracks himself up,
And with every old pun, they can't help but sup.

The symphony swells, a shell-tastic show,
Filled with laughter, as the tides ebb and flow.
In this coastal arena, where joy takes its toll,
A merry parade, the shells rock and roll!

Gentle Ripples of Time

The water whispers, "Hey, let's unwind,"
As fish start to gossip, mingling with kind.
They share silly tales of immense fish size,
And how they once outswam the pooch with the eyes.

An eel with a grin, says "I'm quite the catch!"
With tales of the ones he's sworn to outmatch.
The rockfish all chuckle, "What nonsense you tell!
We know you're just saying, you swim like a snail!"

But laughter's contagious, even the sharks grin,
They join in the merriment, ready to spin.
While waves gently lap at the side of the reef,
Every ripple of joy covers all with belief.

So the ocean keeps chatting, with giggles galore,
In this tranquil abyss, where laughter is stored.
Someone once said, "Time flows like a rhyme,"
And here in the deep, it's always sublime!

Seafarer's Soliloquy

Oh, to sail on a slippery sock,
Where fish wear shades and talk like a rock.
With seagulls squawking, 'Watch your hat!',
I tossed it away, and now it's a brat!

The waves laugh at my tangled hair,
Mighty sharks join in, they don't seem to care.
I balance my lunch on a wobbly plank,
As gulls dive down for a snack, oh, the prank!

My ship is a tub with a fashion faux pas,
Who knew seaweed could be a star?
With barnacles singing a jolly sea tune,
I wonder if mermaids do cartwheels at noon!

So here's to the sea, with its silly songs,
With jellyfish dancing in glittery throngs.
I'll ride on the waves, where mischief is found,
In my nautical dreams, of joy, I'm unbound!

Dreams Drenched in Indigo

Floating in dreams of bright turquoise blue,
I chased a squid, who was wearing a shoe.
With starfish as friends, we danced on the sand,
While crabs played the drums in this goofy band!

The seafoam tickles as I try to float,
A dolphin pops up, wearing a coat.
He winks and he says, "Join my nonsense race!",
With waves as our track, oh, what a wild chase!

I dived for the treasure, but it was just trash,
A rubber duck, oh what a splash!
Yet still, I laughed, 'cause who needs gold,
When you're rich in laughs and stories retold?

In twilight's glow, the sea tells a tale,
Of pirates who lost to a runaway snail.
So let's lift our sails, drink lemonade in glee,
In these dreams where the ocean just lets us be!

Waves Whispering Secrets

Whispers of waves, what could they say?
'Don't wear a swimsuit on the big wave day!'
With a flip and a flop, I took quite a plunge,
Emerging with seaweed like a slippery sponge!

The tides tell stories of fish with a flair,
A grand tale of a crab in a vintage chair.
He sips on his sea tea, feeling quite spry,
While jellyfish giggle and float by the guy!

When dolphins play tag, they've forgotten the rules,
Splashing around like a pack of school fools.
They leap and they spin with such joyful delight,
As I try to avoid being caught in their flight!

So let's toast to the brine and the salty breeze,
To laughter and silliness, oh how they tease!
With waves as our friends and the sun shining bright,
We'll dance in the water until it's night!

Tides of Forgotten Dreams

In dreams where the tide brings a lost rubber duck,
I paddled on waves, oh, what a good luck!
With octopi serving tea in fine hats,
I forgot my swimsuit, and that's where it's at!

The fish play peek-a-boo, calling my name,
I joined in their fun—what a ridiculous game!
With flippers and fins, we twirled on the foam,
Singing off-key, in this watery home!

A pirate appeared, with a parrot that's shy,
He said, 'Want my treasure?' I answered, 'Oh my!
Is it chocolate or pizza, or maybe a shoe?'
He laughed so hard, said, 'Just treasure a few!'

The tide comes in with winks and bright trails,
Under umbrellas that dance like big whales.
So let's ride the tide, where laughter abounds,
In this sea of dreams, where silliness drowns!

www.ingramcontent.com/pod-product-compliance
Lightning Source LLC
Chambersburg PA
CBHW072215070526
44585CB00015B/1343